FLASHBACK TO THE . . .

AWESOME '80s

By Patty Michaels

Illustrated by Sarah Rebar

GLOSSARY

Answering machine: A machine that receives phone calls and lets callers leave a message at the beep

Boom box: A large, portable music player

Camcorder: A combination video and audio recording device

Cordless phone: A wireless, portable phone that receives signals from a station connected to a landline

Floppy disk: A square plastic disk where data from a computer is stored

Gnarly: A slang word for excellent

Mullet: A hairstyle where the hair is short in the front and sides, and long in the back

Perm: A chemical treatment that gives your hair permanent waves or curls

Rad: Another word for cool

Tubular: A word meaning awesome or excellent

VCR (videocassette recorder): An electronic device that plays videocassettes and can also record content from your TV onto them

Walkman: A small, portable music player that can be listened to with headphones. The Sony Walkman was one of the most popular brands of these kinds of music players in the 1980s.

Note to readers: Some of these words may have more than one definition. The definitions above match how these words are used in this book.

CONTENTS

Chapter 1
Totally Trendy!

I ♥ '80s

Let's go traveling back in time,
way back . . . to the awesome 1980s!

Get ready for a totally **tubular** ride as you learn about trends, fads, and other **rad** things that helped define the decade!

Some of the most popular toys were Teddy Ruxpin, Transformers, Rubik's Cube, Cabbage Patch Kids, Simon, and Strawberry Shortcake.

By 1983 almost three million Cabbage Patch Kids had already been adopted!

In addition to playing with these rad toys, kids in the 1980s were also busy with **gnarly** activities like roller-skating, skateboarding, and playing video games at an arcade.

But with the rise of at-home video gaming systems, kids started spending less time at arcades.

Gaming systems like Atari, Nintendo, and Sega Genesis let kids play popular games like Pac-Man, Donkey Kong, Tetris, and Frogger right at home!

The famous inventor and co-founder of Apple, Steve Jobs, once designed video games for Atari, earning five dollars an hour!

When kids weren't playing video games, you might find them listening to music.

You could hear lots of pop and rock songs on the radio, and new genres like rap and hip-hop were becoming bigger and bigger.

The music channel MTV premiered on August 1, 1981, bringing music videos to homes all over the country!

Music in the '80s was best listened to through headphones plugged into a portable cassette player, like the Sony **Walkman**.

Or, even better, you could blast your favorite songs out of a giant **boom box**!

Anyone who grew up in the '80s will remember making homemade mixed cassette tapes by recording songs off the radio.
(And can you believe that back then you had to actually rewind cassette tapes by pressing a button on your radio or stereo?)

You could also manually rewind a cassette tape by using a pen or pencil, *if* you had the time.

TV was pretty different in the '80s too. There weren't nearly as many stations as there are today, and there was definitely no streaming or on-demand viewing.

Many TVs back then didn't come with a remote control, so you had to manually change the channel!

Saturday was *the* best day for kids to watch television. It meant Saturday-morning cartoons! Kids would grab bowls of their favorite cereal and plop in front of the TV to watch popular shows like *The Smurfs*, *Jem and the Holograms*, *He-Man and the Masters of the Universe*, and *Teenage Mutant Ninja Turtles*.

If you wanted to watch your favorite show, you had to watch it at the time it aired.
Luckily, **VCR**s became popular in the 1980s. If you set your timer, you could tape the show and watch it later.

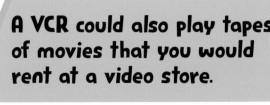

A VCR could also play tapes of movies that you would rent at a video store.

Home **camcorders** became popular too.
Since digital photos and videos
didn't exist yet, this was a great way
for families to record their memories!

Chapter 2
Far-Out Fashion and Fads

When it comes to fashion and style, the 1980s were, like, the coolest decade ever.

Popular hairstyles included **perms**, side ponytails, and teased and crimped hair.

Another popular hairstyle was the **mullet**. It was described as "business in the front, party in the back"!

Neon colors, layered looks with tutus,
tracksuits, bomber jackets,
and leather jackets were some
of the hippest looks of the decade.

Accessories like jelly shoes, scrunchies, fingerless gloves, charm bracelets, giant hair bows, bucket hats, and oversized gold chains were super trendy.
(And some of these trends are once again popular today!)

Jelly shoes became all the rage in America after their debut at the 1982 World's Fair in Knoxville, Tennessee—and the rest is history!

Chapter 3
Say What?

Methods of communication in the 1980s were *way* different than they are today. Take phones, for example.

The days of a phone only connected to a wire were coming to an end. People were psyched to talk on **cordless phones** and leave a message on an **answering machine**.

Alexander Graham Bell was awarded the first patent for an electric telephone in March 1876.

Telephones also looked really fun
in the 1980s.
Some were shaped like
cartoon characters or foods.
You could even see through some
phones!

One of the first cell phones hit stores in 1984. Nicknamed "The Brick," it weighed almost two pounds!

Computers were also very different in the 1980s.
They were large and heavy, and you saved information on a **floppy disk**.

And as far as the internet goes? That was *years* away from being readily available in people's homes!

The GIF image format was invented in 1987, but the engineer who invented it meant for the word to be pronounced "jiff"!

Owning your own computer
was rare during this decade
since they were very expensive.
But you could always go to your local
library to use one.

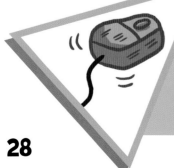

Did you know the first
computer mouse was actually
made of wood?

Typewriters and word processor machines were much more common and affordable.

Back then a word processor was the actual hardware that helped with writing and editing information, not the software programs still used today to create documents, like Microsoft Word.

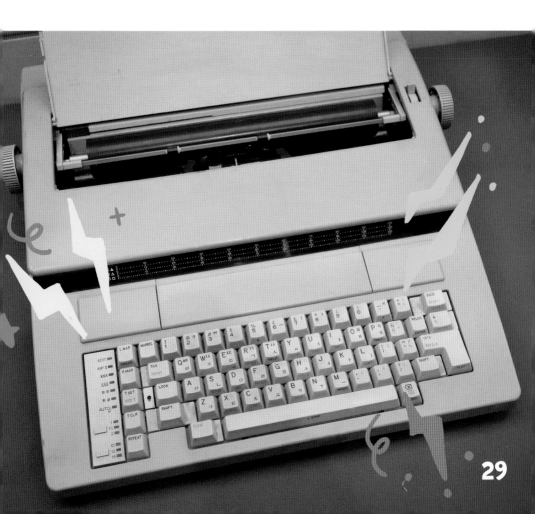

Did you have fun on your awesome
time-traveling adventure?
Weren't the '80s super awesome?

Now that you know a little about what was popular in the 1980s, can you name some things from that decade that are similar today? What things are completely different?

Make Your Own 1980s Time Capsule!

Now that you're an expert on all things from this awesome decade, here's a fun activity that you and a grown-up can do together! Ask them what they remember about the 1980s and if they have any souvenirs they can give you (like a ticket stub, jewelry, or a photo). Then either draw or print out pictures of things that you learned about the decade. Place all of your collected items and pictures in a large plastic jar to create your very own 1980s time capsule that you can display in your room!

FLASHBACK TO THE....

FLY '90s

BY Patty Michaels   ILLUSTRATED BY Sarah Rebar

GLOSSARY

Caller ID: A phone service that shows you the number of the person calling you

Call-waiting: A phone feature that notifies you with a beep when another person is trying to call you while you're currently talking on the phone

CD (compact disc): A small disc containing music or data

Doc Martens: A popular brand of boot-style footwear

Electric Slide: A group dance performed to the song of the same name typically done at weddings and parties

Grunge: A genre of music that reached its height of popularity in the 1990s, incorporating other styles of music, like punk rock and heavy metal

Iconic: A word that means "widely known"

Macarena: A Spanish dance based on a song of the same name

Pager: A small, portable electronic device that beeps or vibrates when someone is trying to reach you

Personal computer (PC): A multipurpose computer designed for individual people to use

Tamagotchi: A small, egg-shaped toy with a screen, containing a digital pet to take care of

Wicked: Another word for "great" or "exceptional"

Note to readers: Some of these words may have more than one definition. The definitions above match how these words are used in this book.

CONTENTS

Chapter 1
Off-the-Chain Trends

Are you ready for an amazing time-traveling adventure?
We are going way back . . .
to the fly 1990s!

Lace up your **Doc Martens** as you learn about fabulous fads, fresh trends, and other majorly cool things that helped define the decade.

Toys in the '90s were off the hook.
Kids loved Beanie Babies,
Tamagotchis (say: Tam-AH-GOT-chees),
Furbies, and Tickle Me Elmo.
The store Build-A-Bear Workshop
debuted in 1997, letting kids make
their own unique stuffed animals!

The Beanie Babies craze began in 1995. The first nine Beanie Babies included a frog, a pig, a lobster, and a platypus!

And home video-gaming systems got more modern with the launch of Nintendo 64 and Sony PlayStation. Sony PlayStation used **CDs** instead of cartridges for its games, which provided *super* high-quality graphics.

CDs were also replacing the way
people listened to music.
Stores like Sam Goody, FYE,
and Tower Records were the
coolest places to check out
CDs from the newest bands.

The first song to ever use Auto-Tune as a sound effect came out in 1998.

Grunge music was popular,
and so were other types,
such as rap, hip-hop, pop,
and music from teen bands.
And everyone was learning new dances
like the **Macarena** and the **Electric Slide!**

When kids weren't listening to the dopest music, they were watching popular '90s TV shows like *Teletubbies*, *Rugrats*, *Barney & Friends*, and *The Powerpuff Girls*.

And anyone who grew up in the 1990s will remember TGIF, which stood for Thank Goodness It's Funny. Families gathered on the couch on Friday nights to watch comedy shows like *Full House* and *Family Matters*.

You might hear people say "TGIF!" That phrase also means "Thank Goodness It's Friday!"

Food and snacks in the '90s
were totally **iconic** (say: eye-CON-ick).
Kids couldn't wait to pack Lunchables
in their backpacks and have Hot
Pockets and Bagel Bites after school.

Funyuns and Dunkaroos were some other popular snacks. And who didn't love a cold and clear Crystal Pepsi to wash it all down?

3D Doritos were introduced in 1998 and were recently re-released in 2020!

Chapter 2
Super-Fresh Fashions and Fads

Fashions and fads of the 1990s were pretty **wicked**. People weren't just listening to grunge music, they were getting inspired to dress in a grunge style, too.

Grunge fashion trends included flannel shirts, ripped jeans, graphic T-shirts, and **Doc Martens**.

Layering sweaters or flannel shirts over T-shirts was a big part of grunge fashion.

If grunge wasn't your style,
you might have been rocking
another popular look of the decade:
cargo pants with a bucket hat.

wow!!

Cargo pants were first
developed by the British
military in 1938.

Another favored trend of the decade was wearing bold colors and patterns, especially geometric patterns and shapes.

Hairstyles of the '90s were *all that* and a bag of chips. Popular styles included pixie cuts, bobs, baby bangs, big curls, flattops, cornrows, and chin-length waves.

Layered hairstyles were all the rage in the '90s. Popular TV shows had characters with layered haircuts, and soon you could see that style everywhere.

Everyone loved accessories
like choker necklaces,
tiny butterfly clips, fanny packs,
and sneakers with pumps in them.
And who didn't have their backpacks
and school supplies decorated
with the colorful art style
of Lisa Frank?

Chapter 3
You've Got Mail!

HOLD, please!

When it comes to the 1990s, nothing changed more than methods of communication.

A **pager** was the coolest device to let you know someone wanted to get in touch with you. And **caller ID** and **call-waiting** on landlines became popular. Now you were not only able to see who was calling you, but also put a call on hold to take another call!

Before call-waiting, if you dialed someone who was already on the phone, you'd hear a busy signal.

Personal cell phones were also becoming more popular.
They were more affordable and smaller than when they were first invented.

A cell phone style known as the "flip phone" was *the* item to have in the '90s.

Popular movies of the '90s started showing characters using cell phones, adding to their popularity!

More and more people started owning **personal computers** (or **PCs**) in the '90s. And many people started using portable PCs (called "laptops").

CDs in the 1990s weren't just used for playing music or video games. Computer programs in the '90s also ran on CDs. CDs also started to phase out floppy disks for data storage.

And the reason why personal computers were becoming so widespread? All because of a little method of communication known as . . . the World Wide Web!

According to statistics from 2022, 63 percent of the world's population uses the Web!

The World Wide Web is an internet
system that allows users to
search for information.
In the 1990s it became available
in homes, libraries, and cafés
across the United States.
People started to "surf the Net"
to look up all sorts of information and
send emails instead of "snail mail"!

Another shift in technology was the creation of AOL (America Online). It was one of the biggest internet service providers in the United States in the 1990s.

AOL was one of the very first companies to tap into the community of the internet, with instant messaging, buddy lists, and online gaming.

In order to access the internet, people would have to dial into the service by using a phone line!

Wasn't that a super-fly
look back at the 1990s?

Now that you know a little about
what was popular in the 1990s,
can you name some things
from that decade that are similar today?
What things are completely different?

Memories in the Making!

Here's a fun 1990s-based activity that'll give you even more insight into this defining decade. Ask a grown-up who lived in the 1990s what their life was like. Did they have a pager or a cell phone? What were their favorite TV shows, and what did they like to wear? And can they describe what the internet was like when it was really just beginning?

FLASHBACK TO THE...
CHILL 2000s!

By Gloria Cruz
Illustrated by Sarah Rebar

GLOSSARY

BlackBerry: A wireless handheld device that allowed users to make phone calls, send emails, and access the Internet

Bling: A word used to describe shiny jewelry

Chillax: A combination of the words "relax" and "chill"

Da bomb: A term used to describe something very cool or awesome

DVD (digital video disc): A disc used to store data like movies and music

Fetch: A word that means "very fashionable"

Heelys: A brand of shoe that features a detachable wheel at the bottom of the heel and can also be used as roller skates

Poppin': A word meaning "cool"

Stoked: Another word for "excited"

Uggs: A style of furry sheepskin boots

Y2K: An acronym for the Year 2000

Note to readers: Some of these words may have more than one definition. The definitions above match how these words are used in this book.

CONTENTS

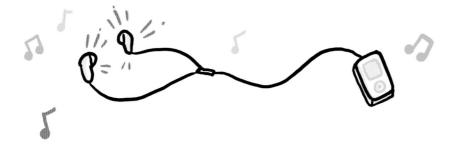

Chapter 1
Totally Rad Trends!

Are you ready
to take a trip back in time?
Lean back and enjoy the chill 2000s!

Put on your favorite pair of **Uggs** as you learn about the **poppin'** trends and fads that totally ruled this decade.

The 2000s had cool toys, like Furbies, Skip-Its, and Sillybandz, and popular dolls, like Bratz and My Scene.

Kids were also **stoked** about the Nintendo Wii gaming system— you'd dance in front of your TV pretending to be a rock star with games like *Just Dance*, *Rock Band*, and *Guitar Hero*!

The Nintendo Wii is Nintendo's most successful home console ever, selling over 100 million units worldwide by 2013!

Music technology in the 2000s was **da bomb.** A device called the iPod was released. It could hold up to a thousand of your favorite songs and even some games!

The iPod Mini was released in 2004, making music even easier to bring on the go!

Music in the 2000s was off the hook! Pop, hip-hop, and country music were some of the most popular musical styles of the decade.

American Idol premiered in 2002, becoming one of the biggest singing competition shows of all time!

Flat-screen TVs became popular, and VHS tapes were being replaced with **DVDs**. People would pick a movie they wanted to watch on Netflix's website and have the DVD mailed to them. (Then they would mail it back.)

Netflix launched its streaming service to consumers in 2007, making it the Netflix we're all familiar with today!

And with TV stations like Disney Channel, Nickelodeon, and Cartoon Network, everyone had a favorite cartoon! Maybe it was *Kim Possible*, *Dora the Explorer*, *Teen Titans*, or *The Powerpuff Girls*.

Popular TV commercials during the 2000s introduced new snacks and drinks being released in super-funky colors.

Heinz ketchup turned
purple and green,
and Pepsi turned blue!

Food trends in the 2000s were anything but **chillaxed**. Eating healthy and organic foods became totally **fetch**!

Annual sales of organic food hit $24 billion by 2009!

But no one could resist the delicious drinks from Starbucks. And you totally had to get extra whipped cream on your Frappuccino!

Chapter 2
Fetch Fashion and Fads

Fashion in the 2000s was epic.
In this decade the **bling**,
footwear, and clothing
trends made very bold statements!

Bling included jewelry
that spelled out your name.
And mood rings and best-friend
charm necklaces were
total must-haves.

If you weren't into jewelry,
then you were probably expressing
yourself through your hairstyle.

Popular hairstyles included
chunky highlights
and cornrow braids.
And some people preferred
spiky hair with lots of hair gel!

Fashion in the 2000s was some of the best yet. Besties couldn't resist wearing matching Juicy Couture sweat suits. Staying comfortable in soft **Uggs** or in baggy clothes was key.

Juicy Couture tracksuits debuted in 2001 and became one of the most popular looks of the decade.

Or, you were probably
walkin' by day and rollin' by night
in your **Heelys**!

Other popular styles
and accessories included
oversized sunglasses,
mini purses,
tiny butterfly hair clips,
and trucker hats.

They were some of *the* trademark accessories during the 2000s!

Chapter 3
Stay Connected!

Types of communication
were on a *whole* new level
with the rise of social media,
which hit its stride in the 2000s.

Websites and games like Myspace, Facebook, and Club Penguin made it possible for people to stay in touch through the Internet. And on a new site called YouTube, anyone could post fun videos of themselves.

Facebook was created in 2004 by a student at Harvard University as a way for all of the students to connect with one another.

Methods of communicating were also totally changing. Gadgets like the **BlackBerry**, the Sidekick, and the iBook made the 2000s a decade to remember!

But one of the most iconic tech
inventions of the 2000s was the iPhone.
It was an iPod and touchscreen
cell phone in one!

OMG

The *iPhone* forever changed
technology and how people
communicated. It allowed users
to listen to music, make phone
calls, send emails, and surf the
Internet—in one device.

And who could forget the rumors about **Y2K**? Since the types of computers we use today were invented in the 1900s, they were programmed to only show two digits instead of four for the year.

Everyone panicked, thinking that when the calendar hit January 1, 2000, (at the turn of the century), computers would go to "00" and all systems would think it was 1900! This was called the "millennium bug."

To solve this problem, the government stepped in, instructing the computer industry to use four digits for years instead of two digits.

Wasn't that time-traveling adventure
all that and a bag of chips?

The 2000s started a lot of the trends we see today. Well, it's time to bounce, so catch you next time!

2000s Throwbacks!

Here's a fun activity you and a grown-up can do together! Ask them if they have any items of clothing that could represent the looks from the 2000s. If they do, try to make some cool outfits of your own that you might have liked to wear if you had grown up in that decade.

Another fun activity you can do is look at old photos from the 2000s. Do you like any of the styles? Do you notice anything similar to what's popular today?

Arf!